PENGUIN BOOKS

ORGANS OF LITTLE IMPORTANCE

Adrienne Chung's poetry and prose have appeared in *The Yale Review*, *Joyland*, *Recliner*, and elsewhere, and have been supported by the Bread Loaf Writers' Conference and the Wisconsin Institute for Creative Writing. She is a graduate of Stanford University and the University of Wisconsin–Madison's MFA program.

The National Poetry Series was established in 1978 to ensure the publication of five collections of poetry annually through five participating publishers. The Series is funded annually by Amazon Literary Partnership, William Geoffrey Beattie, the Gettinger Family Foundation, Bruce Gibney, HarperCollins Publishers, the Stephen and Tabitha King Foundation, Padma Lakshmi, Lannan Foundation, Newman's Own Foundation, Anna and Olafur Olafsson, Penguin Random House, the Poetry Foundation, Amy Tan and Louis DeMattei, Amor Towles, Elise and Steven Trulaske, and the National Poetry Series Board of Directors.

THE NATIONAL POETRY SERIES
WINNERS OF 2022 OPEN COMPETITION

Organs of Little Importance by Adrienne Chung
Chosen by Solmaz Sharif for Penguin Books

Tender Headed by Olatunde Osinaike
Chosen by Camille Rankine for Akashic Books

Survival Strategies by Tennison S. Black
Chosen by Adrienne Su for University of Georgia Press

I Love Information by Courtney Bush
Chosen by Brian Teare for Milkweed Editions

Sweet Movie by Alisha Dietzman
Chosen by Victoria Chang for Beacon Press

ORGANS OF LITTLE IMPORTANCE

ADRIENNE CHUNG

PENGUIN BOOKS

PENGUIN BOOKS
An imprint of Penguin Random House LLC
penguinrandomhouse.com

Page 63 constitutes an extension of this copyright page.

LIBRARY OF CONGRESS CATALOGING-IN-PUBLICATION DATA
Names: Chung, Adrienne, author.
Title: Organs of little importance / Adrienne Chung.
Description: [New York] : Penguin Books, [2023] | Summary: "Taking its
title from Darwin's On the Origin of Species, this debut collection
investigates the theoretically vestigial parts of our
psychologies-residues of first impressions, thought spirals to nowhere,
memories that persist despite outliving their usefulness. Chung collects
and preserves psychological debris as one would care for precious
heirlooms, revealing their surprising potential as sites of meaning and
connection"—Provided by publisher.
Identifiers: LCCN 2023018234 | ISBN 9780143137740 (trade paperback) |
ISBN 9780593511862 (ebook)
Subjects: LCGFT: Poetry.
Classification: LCC PS3603.H8526 O74 2023 |
DDC 811/.6—dc23/eng/20230526
LC record available at https://lccn.loc.gov/2023018234

Printed in the United States of America
1st Printing

Set in Perpetua MT Pro
Designed by Sabrina Bowers

"I have sometimes felt great difficulty in understanding the origin or formation of parts of little importance . . ."

CHARLES DARWIN,
On the Origin of Species

"If you want my future, forget my past."

SPICE GIRLS,
"Wannabe"

Contents

ORGANS OF LITTLE IMPORTANCE

Tasman

It was summer in Berlin. I wore a dress of white muslin.
I slept by the window, draped in Mennonite muslin.

In a hostel I met an Australian named Tasman.
Two weeks of heaven, smeared marmite on muslin.

When Tasman went home, I pleaded with heaven.
Night hung low in the branches, twilight muslin.

Why is there always that scene in the movies—
white sheets on clotheslines, rippling like muslin?

My mother prayed for a girl in pink satin.
God punished her with a small fright in muslin.

She loved me so much that she slapped me and singed me.
In the morning I bandaged my eyes in tight muslin.

I understood. No one's perfect—even Plath
could have called it a lampshade of bright muslin.

I chased the moon. I howled for my Tasman.
I stumbled through brambles in a dress of sliced muslin.

The next morning, I arrived at a clearing. The trees
had pale leaves, like they might be muslin.

Look where you are, Adrienne, it's just like the movies—
white flags around you, rippling like muslin.

Bardo Baby

I've talked to trees, had long-winded conversations about thrownness with Japanese maples,
talked to redwoods about hydration, macronutrients, love languages, relatives down south, how
      some trees miss me when I'm gone and
      some trees shiver like a spineless creature, dickmatized, and
      some trees glitter in the dark, leaves like gold sequins, silver sequins, red sequins,
         orange sequins

Once I swiped left on a man who wrote *I love rollercoaster, fresh-squished orange juice*
I was youngish then, eyes unopened to the world's hidden glam
Eight years later I lie in bed fantasizing about what he didn't list,
      how he likes his martini, his hand job, his pizza, the permutation of his linens,
      how he'd misspell *strudel, Nietzsche, Mississippi, Klingon, onomatopoeia,*
      how he might have loved me but

It was more difficult that year to hear *I love you* than to say it, words kneading
like the angry knobs of my grandmother's massage chair where she sat every night, upright
as the handsome older woman that I cannot stop myself from becoming

It isn't that I'm mad about being flat-chested, more like gracefully annoyed
with the procedure of mammograms, my small breasts flattened like paninis every January,
the technician groping my chest with the torque of a bleary-eyed, open-mouthed lover who
    rolls over
after the small fireworks of anonymous sex while at night I dream on Egyptian cotton
of dead elephants suspended like dried flowers from the ceiling of my mother's bedroom

My Jungian analyst says that a part of my heart is dead and this hurts me
I conjure a colorless sky and this calms me until I look out the window
where a blue curtain hangs spherical from the firmament
      Why am I still scared of demons and loud noises, of my reflection in the mirror?
      Why am I every age at once, each part of my body frozen in a different time?
         Baby face, grandma hands, toddler butt, teenie tits

I didn't know that my mother had 36DDs when I sat alone in the waiting room
popping reams of bubble wrap while a radiation machine zapped her breasts
That year I was six and loved dolls with a selfless desire,
      the way dogs love humans, unconditionally and without interiority
      the way I loved my mother, unconditionally and without interiority

She tried to lose me but each time I found her
One second I was fingering the hairy back of a peach and the next she was gone,
the cloud of her absence a ghostly imprint between the jars of soy sauce and peanut oil,
the branded void into which my heart would drop when I realized she was gone
Each time I was ready to end my little life, to follow her into whatever darkness of her
  condemnation

The first time I heard my mother called a psychopath was like a hit of cocaine,
a flash of white, a reel of film where every character from every life I've ever lived
rushes back into the brain, packing the red carpet of memory's ballroom into which I emerge,
a debutante, twirling down the coiled staircase with the garish ceremony of childbirth
  Hello! Here I am! I say, my teeth smeared with the lurid pink lipstick of 1985

I was born in November, a Valentine's baby, Scorpio monstrosity,
Chinese finger trap, overweight firstborn, hirsute mandarin,
small-mouthed delicacy, Hunan princess, sentient Bratz doll,
boba dowager, purebred powerbottom, moonfaced cowgirl,
  doomed to cheat, doomed to lie,
  doomed to steal, doomed to die

I think I'm in love again with the only man who ever loved me
He was named for a saint, first of the apostles
I couldn't imagine ever loving him again but suddenly I found God and in Him I saw something,
  something old, something new, something borrowed,
  something—

Once, under a bright blue sky, she left me
I counted gummy bears in the clouds, sang Disney songs to myself
until the white stitch screeched and pulled apart, begat a bloodied black dome, pulsing
I cried to the trees but they couldn't help me, so I sang to the trees but they couldn't hear me,
the straps of the car seat sustaining my little body like the tubes of a ventilator

Does something remain ill-fated if it has already met its fate?
Does the sickness abandon course or does it live on like a phantom limb, atmospheric,
like a virus on a ghost ship where immortality is less a paradise than a human zoo

Again I wake up as if there were no possibility of dying
Again I scroll through political news in bed, open my email where still shelved beneath his name
  in Gchat are his final words: *I can't sleep*
Again I dress myself, feed myself, carve sex appeal into my face so that when a beautiful man looks

at me, my skull floods with the histrionic strings of Vivaldi like a drug, yet
        still I'm afraid of looking behind me
        still I'm afraid of closing my eyes
        still I'm afraid of the past, present, and future, but

She was always there
        a hundred times
I was ready to die
        a thousand times
Each time she saved me
        a baker's dozen million times

An angel, ghostlit fantasy, appearing in the final dark.

La Sagra

We learned the word
for holiday. We went around
the room, each naming one.
I said Chinese New Year.
Someone said Halloween.
Then someone said hayrides
at the pumpkin patch
and I imagined myself
on the back of a truck
at dusk, a little drunk
and laughing, knocking
into the side of the wagon
as it swung around
bales of hay. Gold filaments
in the sky like rain.
Who is this small child
at my side? I look at her,
intently because she looks
like me, then at the man
next to her whom I no longer
know. Moonlight binds
our hands in a straight line
from heaven to earth.
Someone says Thanksgiving.
Someone says Christmas.
Christmas with your parents,
Easter with your friends,
says the teacher. I have friends
I don't spend Easter with,
parents who don't know
my name. I've never dreamed
of a family before, of a lover
and a child in the same scene.

Duty-Free

My mother lives in hotel rooms amidst
unopened boxes of perfumes and creams
and purses, the shrink-wrap glinting off her face
like glitter on a child's. She sleeps among her towers
of Chanel, Celine, McQueen—she has no other lovers,
only me because I call her. Now I get no answer.
The phone bills pile higher.
On Christmases she gave me plastic bags
of drugstore loot: dishwashing gloves in pink
and purple, blue nail polish with a glimmer.
I wore the gloves as soon as I returned
from school each day. This was how
I loved her: devotion to a specter.
She loved midnight runs to Walgreens,
leaving me alone and frightened.
Now I'm thirty and still fearful
that a man will come at night
but I don't blame her for my fear of sleep
and dreams without a mother.
Mornings I'd awake to bags of booty
at the door. I can see her drop them
in a hurry, evade one mirror, then another,
run to sate her shame with pills which put her out
before I saw her. I have no memories
of this mother. All I wanted was a mother.

OHNE TITEL

In Jungian analysis, dreams are meticulously recounted and dissected, titled as if they are of cinematic importance. Freud called them *the royal road to the unconscious*. In my dreams, I lose my hair.[1] Sometimes there are people present but I don't know who they are and I don't question the question of their identity. In my dreams, people die[2] and my lover's father commits adultery.[3] Freud believed that every dream has a connection point with an experience of the previous day. In my dreams, I have killed a woman and hidden her body in a room for days.

---

[1] *The Time Is 11:24*: I'm losing my hair, the right side of my head crosshatched like a checkerboard. I walk down the cobblestone street in the French quarter of Shanghai, tall willows grazing my scalp.

[2] *The Game*: The house is under invasion. I escape through a small window above the toilet. I then find myself in the hallway of a large dormitory, where I walk uninvited through a door. On the other side, a woman and I frantically look for a phone, rummaging through the room for days until finally she pulls out from underneath her arm, like a baguette, a large ziplock bag containing a cell phone. She frowns as if to say that she is disappointed that we had to resort to this backup, as if we'd lost some sort of game. We call the police, though by then it was too late and someone had been killed.

[3] *Call the Doctor*: His father took house calls with women, inching his stethoscope up their thighs.

Freud liked how cocaine made him feel, how it opened the floodgates of the mind, letting the locked thoughts spill out like the light from a lab of synthetic diamonds. Have you ever read Freud on cocaine? Have you ever felt epically nauseated by the spell of oxygen in this world? Have you ever dreamed something so profane that it could only have come from your own mind? In my dreams, people die.[4]

---

[4] *Do I Still Love Him?*: My mother once told me that when you're near a window and your arm suddenly feels electric, you're about to die. In the back of a taxicab, I ask if I can hold him. He says yes. I embrace him with my whole body, knowing that he is already dead.

My analyst is seventy-three. Because he went to military school and is still married to the mother of his three children, I put my blind faith in him to lead me out of the dark. At our first session, he tells me to exercise and meditate. At our second session, I tell him about a dream where a metal beam sliced my head off its body. He was a green snail, watching from the ground. The next morning, I put on a green shirt as if something happened.

Freud says that dreams are the fulfillment of a wish. I dream that a former Food Network chef is my mother.[5] I dream about attachment to men who love me.[6] I dream about happy times with my mother.[7] I dream about crying because I can't in waking life. I stare at a white wall until I dream again.

---

[5] *Giada's Stomach*: I arrive at my massage appointment in a peach-colored suburban tract home of the sort that popped up in droves in the late nineties in California. The masseuse is late. I wait and wait and end up falling asleep overnight in an empty room. In the morning I begin to feel lonely. I walk around the house looking for another human and find Giada De Laurentiis. Her body, impossibly tan and concave on television, is pale and full before me. I can't see her face from beneath the milky white balloon of her abdomen, with which I am eye level. Scientific illustrations of the uterus and ovaries suddenly appear on her stomach in bright purples and greens, as if from a textbook. I press my wet cheek to her stomach.

[6] *X*: The instructor is disappointed with me because I am out of practice and unable to re-member choreography. Suddenly I'm high up in a tree and looking through the window into a martial arts class. I recognize one of the men in the class. He is very good, which surprises me. I find it very attractive.

[7] *Almost Dead*: My mother looks like she did in her forties, when she was still hilarious and vivacious, when we were at the height of our enmity. She explains that the secret ingredient to curry is wheat germ, something she parroted as a health food until it became too gluten-ous and almost killed her. She hated when I corrected her.

Sometimes my analyst is wrong. He advises me to contact a childhood friend who appears in my dream.[8] I find her on Facebook and we meet for wine once and never again, the mutual dreaming more a dream than the dream itself. He tells me to grieve but I promised myself this year that I would wear color.[9]

---

[8] *Stalker*: I'm in a car and C is driving. In the back, her father sits tall and handsome. She misses on-ramps as she tries to get on the highway, speeding down a back road which suddenly ends at a cliff. We fly off into the forested abyss, the trees coming alive with color as we plummet. When we land, the two of us are unharmed. I think to myself how terrible it would be if I were the sole survivor and had to find my way out alone.

[9] *Jim Carrey's* The Mask: I am driving through my old college campus. The winding road forks, then winds more tightly than I can drive. People lie on the grass reading books. I almost crash into a man purposefully stretching in the middle of the road. It's an entitled skateboarder. No one believes that he didn't mean it. I go to class. I'm now on an old bicycle that an old boyfriend built for me when I was twenty-three. I have difficulty finding my classroom and accidentally open the door to a post-op recovery room housing dozens of octogenarians in beds lined up like sardines. I then run into another old boyfriend. He is wearing a bright yellow suit with a purple tie and his facial hair is styled into an embarrassing Hitler-style mustache. He tells me to come back and visit him and that he will shave his mustache if I'd like. I don't have an answer for him.

Eighteen months later, I move three thousand miles away, and not for love. One autumn day I come across a glass snail in a thrift store, the sculpted shell on its back peacocked like a young woman at a party. I deliberate the three-dollar purchase, turning the trinket over in my hands as the heartland sun disappears behind me. Do I need this? Do I *need* this? That week I learned about a recently received poetic form called the egg, its seven lines of ten syllables each mirroring the nutritional perfection of its macros, no more and no less.[10]

---

[10] *Ohne Titel*: I am walking to or from home when out of the corner of my eye, I see a white egg-shaped microwave sitting on a picnic table.

I open my diary. *Black, blu, blau, black. Black, black, black.*

In waking life, I bought the snail. I cried over A. I cried over B. I cried until I had cried over all the men for whom my letters made no difference when I said I would eat less meat, drink less. I would sing less, wear less black. A red scarf, blue socks. A blue scarf, blue socks. Do you remember when recursion was a beautiful thing? We watched one another come over and over that summer.

The Stenographer

I have no house cat, no TV, no lover
I can touch. I sing a song
in a house inside my head and imagine
children sitting around me,
watching in the dark.

Some nights I'm scared
I won't be able to sing.
No song but the whir of a fan
half-circling in the bedroom corner
where in my dreams

I'm in a valley looking up at the sky,
alien angles of a desert sunset
sparkling violet and bright green,
the line between that world
and this one invisible as an ending
where pain would be not punishment
but reprieve.

I have not been visible now for a while.

I slipped between the hours, barely touching
the surface of my life.

Time chased me, passing audibly
in the winter. Scratch of an ice skate
circling over the neon buzz

of the Hy-Vee. I was trailed
by a beer can in a lake,
shadow of a plane over cornfields,
true blue beauty

of a Midwestern sunset, landlocked
and unburdened by freedom.

Reeds swaying on the bank
as though it were some other place.

Arrangements

First we installed a tall white cabinet
and filled it with books, records, a cracked vase
we found in Crete.
You said you liked things the way
I did. So did I.
Quickly we added a table, chairs, lamps, then a desk, until
we had no more room for a sofa, but I supposed
we weren't sofa people anyway.
You agreed. I took your hand
as we stood on the curb and watched the sky
turn from blue to black.

In that certain light I can see again
all the base configurations we attempted
as we tried to think our way out of this
and then that, one light bulb burning out after another
until it was noon again.

Neither of us knew what to do,
so we sold the cabinet
and bought a sofa. It's been months now
and still the books lie open on the wooden floor,
the pages sailing out like moths
in the dark.

Y2K

Bluish dusk of a new millennium and I loved him, though I knew better than what I thought I didn't know, in that I might have loved him for who he was—or wasn't—how was I supposed to know? The origin of primal ooze was nowhere to be found. In history class there was a crying girl whose mother worked in the Twin Towers. We watched her vomit on the linoleum floor before she was taken away to the nurse. The rest of us didn't know how to act or that George W. Bush was a hobbyist painter. On the television, a newscaster's lipstick bled in tendrils across her face. Twenty years later, a boy in a shirt that read DRINK WISCONSINBLY raised a fleshy palm. *If someone's not doing anything with his life and honestly says he's happy, who is Aristotle to say he's not?* I couldn't tell which subreddit had blighted him or whether he looked thirty-five or ten. I text a friend two thousand miles away to say that I miss the good old days in California, where we ate chicken nuggets and applesauce, then ran onto the blacktop screaming, how we shot our arms into the tetherball's vortex, trapping our fingers against the steel pole, hands pulsing hot and bleeding as we watched the O. J. Simpson trial in class.

Feral Spice

At a stoplight, I witness a man in jeans cross paths with another on his morning
run. After a brief bro-down, they run off together into the San Francisco
fog like two golden retrievers.

Not a block later, I pass a red van loudly inscribed with WHO LET THE DOGS OUT?
in the appropriate typeface.

I almost take a photo but cannot summon that thing which compels me to act.

My analyst asks when I first noticed the pattern.

What pattern? I ask, before I realize that he means my pattern of misfortune.

How nice of him. I'd always called it fate.

Well, I say, Tibetan Buddhists believe that preceding a person's birth, the soul
wanders through an infinite plane of naked couples copulating. It stops
when it finds its match and then, presumably, steps between their genitals
and—

A human is born, into the fate it chose.

No—I meant pattern. Yes, I first noticed the pattern late last year when I
sustained two car accidents in as many months. But really, I say, it began in
that infinite plane before I was born, and—

Yes, I can see why I chose this pattern, why I chose to spend my childhood
alone, watching cartoons from morning till night, eating bowls of Grape-
Nuts in nothing but water, the little seeds cutting into my four-year-old gums
until finally the sun set and my mother woke up.

My analyst tells me that I must learn to mother myself but I have already begun
talking to my houseplants.

On the way home, I stop to pet two dogs in hopes of activating a triplicate canine
synchronicity.

Later, I have a beautiful bowel movement and recklessly sage my apartment, nearly setting a blanket, then a book, on fire.

Say I chose this.

I strip naked in front of a window in darkness. I turn over a mousetrap to look at the dead body, its white belly soft and distended beyond proportion. I wanted to touch it.

In the distance, the Golden Gate Bridge arcs toward the hills of Marin County, where two friends once cast me as "Feral Spice" in a music video. They drew red scars down my cheeks and gave me a baseball bat wrapped in barbed wire.

You're half-feral, half-domesticated, they explained.

I ran through thorny acacia bushes in a dense machine-generated fog, swinging the bat at the sky.

What if I said I touched it—

What if I said I waited all night for another to snap.

Problem

I.

1. Upon further examination

    A. I have confirmed that

        i. My vanity is a result of neuroticism rather than a need for attention. The seed of my rationale is that the definitive categorization of a thing renders it dead, its placement in the metaphysical grid an imprisonment, a life sentence in which a life sentence is a death sentence.

        Categorization is a dismissal, a flattening, an end stop to the evolution of a thing, the tombstone which marks its place in the graveyard of things taxidermied by taxonomization.

        Do you understand where I am going with this?

        When you say I am beautiful, you are killing me. Yet when you are killing me, you are remembering me because the nature of beauty is that it asks to be reproduced. Because I am beautiful, you want to look at me

        and look at me repeatedly, to capture me again and again until I am no longer there and you cannot

        look at me and you must remember me, conjuring me with each blink of the mind's eye, the facsimile of my perfect body multiplying through time and space.
Thus   beauty is
simultaneously an obliteration and assertion of the self, its death and life synthesized and sublimated into an endlessly recurring resurrection such that at any moment I am occupying three parallel existential planes:

I am dead and I am alive and I am resurrected

while I am dead and I am alive and I am resurrected.

        Thus you will remember me each time you forget me.   May you remember me
as you forget me as you remember me as you forget me as you remember me as you forget—

II.

In *An Enquiry Concerning Human Understanding*, Hume makes the distinction between events that are conjoined and those that are connected.[1] Connection, according to Hume, necessitates a relation of causation,[2] where *If P, Then Q*; where *If Not Now, Then Never*; where *If So, Then Why Me?* as if a causal relation were the measure of truth which determined whether a thing were truly connected or simply conjoined to another. Body and soul are theoretically conjoined and connected in physical and psychic unity. Twins conjoined at the hip in eternal enmity are conjoined but not connected. Two teenage boys double-dared to superglue their naked asses to each other are conjoined but not connected, their bovine eyes peering blankly toward opposite ends of the earth.

But who are we to say that these two boys were not connected at some point in time? That there was not once a connection in which they looked in the same metaphysical distance and saw the same light across the water, which told them to find each other and conjoin themselves in such a manner that could only be undone by WD-40 and public humiliation? In which to unconjoin they must first, or again, connect. Could it be that Hume's fundamental mistake lies in his overlooking of the primordial sympathy that links the conjoined with the connected in its own causal relation? Where in order to be conjoined, two events must have at some point been connected. Where the thin joint of connection conjoined the Möbius loop of space-time. Where you and I with our open mouths pressed together in our own private screams, choral bleat of our uvulas deadened by dank air, conjoined beyond connection.

---

[1] David Hume, *An Enquiry Concerning Human Understanding* (1748), 7.2.58.

[2] Ibid., 7.2.59.

Diptych

I. Date with Dasein

I met a man who gazed too deeply at
a bloody steak and fainted, falling on
the marble floor, his brain a vat of fat
which seeped into the porous stone, a fawn
prostrated on the mythic loam of Whole
Foods, Berkeley: NIMBY-land par excellence.
He could not work for months, the fiscal toll
of mortal coil, but still he danced the danse
macabre—he tapped and swipeth left and right,
received his paycheck from his bed. The life
of one so dumb and masc—what earthen fright
could steak design, awaking such lame strife?
Perhaps he died an ego death and shat
his mind, for in that steak he saw his soul.

II. Love to Travel

If by love you mean the bourgeois ache
for life beyond the nine-to-five of Outlook and
Excel and if by travel, which I take
to mean the Allbirds-padded trek of routes
sophomoric and reviewed on Yelp, then yes,
I understand the provenance of your soul's
ambition for commission trophies lest
your empty shelves remind you of the holes
that dot like lace your hitherto embrace
of life and love and laughter for the likes,
your beignets topped with foie, a demi-glace
of middle-class aspartame which strikes
eventually the brain: the fate of fake
enrichment, cloud of photos at your grave.

Ceremony

How many permutations of first cousins none removed could there possibly be? I asked the photographer if time were a string or a bowl of pearls because I happened to think of it actually as a beach, its blond baubles crushed and raked along the coastline, Zen garden of relativity. When I understood that she did not understand me at all, I left and pornographically cried in the terra-cotta-tiled bathroom, the door to which did not open onto a moonlit balcony where a handsome man stood smoking a cigarette, with sex appeal and feeling. I reentered instead into a scene whose great distance from my adulthood I give daily thanks for but which I was, at the time, condemned to for eternity. I was wearing a long dress. The night's stars were hidden by a blond babel hovering like the false ceiling of an office building. I sat at a long table of people whose way of life I mutually did not respect and whose index fingers did not point correctly down the fork and knife which split open the meat. I opened my third eye in desperation. I took three small steps in the direction of the North Star before resigning to my seat, where I pressed an imaginary finger to my prefrontal cortex and rubbed furiously in small circles to the thought of running away until I achieved orgasm in front of everyone I hated, the burst brilliant and adamantine as diamonds. Once a spiritualist whom I met on a dating site told me that one orgasm on the astral plane is equivalent to ten thousand orgasms on Earth occurring simultaneously in every cell of your body. How could I believe him? How could I not?

Perfect

So that I cannot forget you even as I'm sleeping, I have devised
        a system which establishes in me the object permanence
you so desire in which the number of hours before the sunset
        of our affair is divided by my age in days. Visualized
as a blue cube, for crystallinity, the value is further divided
        six times, once for each of its faces, by the difference
of the eleventh digit of our internet protocol addresses.
        Should the resultant value be of odd denomination,
let the degree of axial asymmetry refract upon it the hue
        of its corresponding hex code such that one face of it
achieves an opacity cloudy as the smoke of our irreconcilable
        difference. In the event that it is even, it appears
that I seem to have kept my promise to always remember
        the hollow of your hand, forever and just   sliding out of mine.

Blindness Pattern

>>

1. There is a mathematical formula $\{ R = e^{-t/s} \}$ which plots the erosion of memory over time, where *Retrievability* is *Euler's number* to the negative power of *Time* over the *Stability of memory*. They call this the Forgetting Curve.

2. What this means is that memory fades.

3. Red is—

    3.1   the dim goading of an Outback Steakhouse

    3.2   the color of the scarf wrapped around Isadora Duncan's neck at one end and entangled in the open-spoked wheels of her car at the other. *Je vais à l'amour*, she said, before snapping her neck in two.

4. Color blindness afflicts men at a rate several times that of women. The most common form is dichromatism, the confusion of red and green. Dichromats have difficulty distinguishing a Braeburn apple from a Granny Smith, the grids of a tartan plaid, a green from a red light.

5. (How unsurprising is it, then, that they have such difficulty distinguishing between *stop* and *go*?)

6. My mother wore Yves Saint Laurent Rouge Pur Couture 7, a waxy magenta lipstick that swiveled out of a four-sided gold tube like an art deco rendition of an Egyptian talisman. She was always late and so it was only in the seconds before exiting the car after a mad drive across the city that she would smear rouge over her lips and dot it across her cheeks, frantically smudging the pigment up toward her temples to paint that startling pink streak so emblematic of the eighties. Sometimes she'd do the same to me, turning me into the same garish creature that I would spend the next twenty years trying to shed.

7. In 1986, a sixty-five-year-old painter wrote to the late neurologist Oliver Sacks complaining of total color blindness after a concussion sustained when a truck rammed into the side of his car. In the months that followed, the world receded. Azure sky and white clouds flattened into a dull gray, tomatoes a dead black, his wife's flesh the color of a rat. Painting became impossible; sex, revolting.

8. Blood splashes a lifeless black on cyan, the vivid blue-green of hospital scrubs. This is no accident. At some point they'd decided that splatters of red on white were tawdry.

9. In the beginning of our courtship, he sent me a photo of an arteriovenous malformation that he had operated on that day. The dark tangle of veins, whose rupture earlier that month had nearly killed the twenty-three-year-old patient, sat flatly on top of the brain. I marveled at its fatty pinkness, framed by the bony white border of skull. The scalp, peeled back and pinned down, was visible along the periphery. A friend asked if this was the neurosurgeon's equivalent of a dick pic. I said *probably*—both brain and dick are pink, soft, and full of the same blood that splashes a dull black on cyan.

>>

1. Retrieval-induced forgetting is a process by which retrieving an item from long-term memory impairs subsequent recall of related items. This is to say that the more we remember, the more we forget.

2. Sometimes I saw it only in memories, in the lonely light of looking back. *That was blue*, I'd remember—*that yellow house was blue*, as if an affliction of a reverse color blindness of blue.

3. When I was three, my uncle taught me how to operate the VHS machine in my bedroom by counting the buttons: five from left was PLAY, four was REW, three was EJECT. I spent much of waking life as a toddler watching and rewatching

my small collection of Disney tapes: *Snow White*, *Bambi*, *Pinocchio*, *Cinderella*, *Lady and the Tramp*, *Alice in Wonderland*, *The Sword in the Stone*, *Fantasia*—though this one I seldom watched, as I hated those menacing brooms dancing in formation. Alone in my room, I watched my tapes from morning till night.

My favorite among them was about the girl who pricked her finger on a spindle and fell asleep for a hundred years, the one with hair down to her waist and a long, narrow face that even then I understood was beautiful. My own hair was kept very short, like a boy's, until grade school. Even now I recall the rage of seeing little girls everywhere with long hair. That rage never left me.

4. Three weeks ago someone told me that my hair looked different. I knew what he meant because I'd noticed, too, because half of postpartum and post-abortive women report some degree of hair loss; because I'd been having anxiety attacks about it, staying up until all hours of the night peering at my scalp like a lunatic. Moments when I snapped out of the hysterical daze and saw my horrible reflection in the mirror—mouth agape, eyes bulging, fistfuls of hair in each hand—I thought, *Medusa*. Medusa, the woman raped by Poseidon, then punished for it, transformed by Athena into a creature so terrible to behold that her mere glance turned men to stone. Because it was her hair and body that tempted him, it was her hair and body that were condemned. What injustice wrought upon her, betrayed by her own body! Medusa, that awful face of feminine rage, looked back at me night after night in the bathroom mirror.

5. Every day I slipped that tape into the VHS machine and followed Aurora from birth through childhood to her fateful sixteenth birthday, when she pricked her finger on that spindle. I watched her sleep in a high blue room. I watched dark vines spread over her castle in irreversible nightfall. I watched Prince Phillip hack through brambles to kiss his comatose beauty. I watched all of this, every day, just to get to my favorite scene at the end: Aurora

and Phillip, now married, waltz across the palace floor as it dissolves, giving way to a blanket of clouds. The three fairies—Flora, Fauna, and Merryweather—look on from above, waving their wands to the beat of Tchaikovsky's "Grande valse villageoise." With each triplet, the clouds and Aurora's dress change from pink to blue and back again, on and on for thirty seconds, until the animation miniaturizes, descending neatly into the background as a leather-bound book cover closes shut. This was how I knew the story was real.

6. Color blindness can also be acquired from a blunt trauma to the head.

7. For two years, I lived with, loved, and submitted to someone who told me, repeatedly, to *stop thinking so much*, to leave the gray for the green. But then what? The present is little more than a fleshy hologram which distorts on sight and disperses on contact: an insipid flicker, a noon shadow.

8. One August morning I stepped out under the harsh glare of Teutonic light to a searing pain in my left eye, as if singed with acid. I collapsed onto the pavement. At the hospital, the ophthalmologists chastised me, grew angry when I apologized for what I'd done to myself. I stayed in a lightless room for the two weeks following, the curtains drawn, as my eye healed from the corneal abrasion.

9. When Joni Mitchell was nine, she contracted polio and was quarantined in a hospital, strapped to a bed and immobilized as it was believed that any movement might cause the disease to spread. She remained alone in that room, stiff on her back, for several months. Was this when she began seeing blue?

That summer I found myself playing *Blue* in my car over and over, not because I liked her shrill voice but because I didn't know why I did, until one day I heard the words

I am a lonely painter

and suddenly I understood.

>>

1. There are memories of specificity and memories of multiplicity which bleed into one another like an endless film reel, flickering to an unknown rhythm. Ghosts tripping the wires, the vague dread of standing at the curb long after all the other children had gone home. I can recall clearly looking down the open road, how the sky at that hour so quickly darkened from blue to black.

2. Darkness is the balm, that which softens the world's hard edges. Out the window, our stalks of amaranth shot up like jeweled bullets.

3. There is a name for the color seen by the mind's eye in perfect darkness, that off-black of an almost-absence. They call this *Eigengrau*:

    3.1 An austere life of hard rules and dry complexions set to minimal techno and a strict schedule of sandwiches on hard, dry breads.

    3.2 He said this was his favorite color.

    I said, *You're a pretentious fuck.*

4. In 1999, a man named Nicholas White was stuck in an elevator for forty-one hours with no phone, watch, or water. Consider that humans can expect to live about three days, or seventy-two hours, without water. At forty-one hours, he was more than halfway to death's door. Whatever happened to him inside that elevator led to the loss of his relationship, job, apartment, and all of his life savings.

5. Do They Know That in China:

    5.1 a *yellow movie* is a pornographic movie and—

    5.2 only members of the imperial household could wear yellow, the color of royalty, and—

    5.3 the first emperor was called the Yellow Emperor

and—

5.4 the last emperor, Puyi, was carefully raised
with only yellow objects surrounding him as
a child? In his memoirs, he recounts, *It made
me understand from my most tender age that I
was of a unique essence, and it instilled in me the
consciousness of my "celestial nature" which made me
different from every other human.*

6. For the seven days following my abortion, I boiled seven
dates in milk nightly until their bodies distended and
dissolved into a curdled ambrosia, tinged yellow by a
spoonful of turmeric. Alone in my apartment, I stirred
this sludge with a wooden spoon and drank it with the
formless conviction that some would call hope. I'd wanted
something *more*—something esoteric, something pagan.
Looking back, I wanted something magical.

7. At some point, I'd begun to see blue where it did not exist
as it was. First I saw it in burgundies because I knew that
the mystery of its purply scarlet was born from a tinge
of blue. Then I saw it in whites simply because I knew it
was there. I saw it in black when it shimmered to a near
navy in sunlight and in the striations of wood because I
imagined that once a blue-eyed woman cast her gaze on
it. I saw it in the concrete slabs downtown, which hid
hundreds of people inside wearing blue as if blue were
something they could take off.

8. Cavafy asks,

   How long can I let my mind moulder in this place?

9. After the amaranth, chive blossoms sprouted in their place,
little heads of periwinkle peeping from the window box.
I didn't remember planting them, or I didn't know they'd
bloom. We shouldn't have. It was a mistake.

   So I let them die, too.

>>

Poetics

Aristotle divided words into categories.
Strange words are foreign, like 水 for water.

Current words are simply ordinary, like water,
blue silk of separation. This is *metaphorical*:

there is nothing between us but a love
now *contracted*: I love*d* him. Or is it *strange*?

What are we allotted if we don't know
the word, having come from another country,

not knowing to inflect a thing that's gone?
Lengthen *love* to *lovingly* and it is *lengthened*,

no longer *strange* because I tend my garden, lovingly,
and know the fruits of love's labor, the metaphor

of water for attention when I prune pale leaves
and sing to flowers in glossolalia,

string of *new* words never before spoken,
unseen and unread, named

for the second before said. Why bother?
I'll never be a virgin again.

Give me *altered* words: part *new*, a collage
because I can't paint. Cut flowers, cut letters

for a ransom note to God.
Cut away the *ornamental*, the unnecessary,

the bloat, the poet's fear. Love handles
no love. Erase everything and begin again.

Punishment

One day hundreds of longboats appeared along the coastline.

There was little time to gather our belongings.

Above us a storm cloud brewed with precision, like music.

I took inventory of the livestock.

I pressed a yellow flower against my eye.

We ran for eighteen months, marauders at our backs.

Nothing could have prepared us for the new land, where even lives were valued.

Here, the reach of my authority was restricted to our bodies.

We believed in science, the difference between necessity and truth.

We believed that executioners could not be Christians.

Here, there were only two kinds of killing: open-handed and stealth.

To hide a thing is to admit its mistake.

I counted five punitive events between us.

To hide a thing is to admit its mistake.

Six.

Ecstatic conditions can sometimes take sadistic forms.

Sadistic conditions often result in ecstatic forms.

Game of manners. Game of cruelty.

Now you love me.

21st Century Pizza

I was seduced through a window one night
by a man in a large black headset, miming a waltz
in an empty gaming parlor. Rain fell
as I huddled under the frame like a stray,
waiting for a world to open
through a door.

For five minutes, I could work for free
in a sandwich shop, a pet store,
or a pizzeria, which I chose by accident
as he placed the headset onto me,
tightening the straps and asking
if I was OK.

I was OK, but possibly unprepared,
something for which I am prepared due to a life
of frequent relocation, general misfortune,
and poor choices in love . . .

There was a pizza shop on Geary
that gave children little balls of pizza dough
to knead to pass the time,
clumps of dampened flour

soft as actual angels
in my hands.

From that day on, I craved
its supple pliancy, how it yearned
for the empty spaces
between my fingers.
I dreamed of its meat, its sweetness
in my mouth.

Years later, when I came home,
no one remembered such a place, dark and narrow
in my mind's eye, dusted in the fine flour
of memory's electric powder.

There was no photo, no witness,
no evidence to burn

because nothing is real here
except me.

Fragment of a Vessel

It was summer. We were young,
or at least I said I was, though I wasn't,
and hadn't been for years. I thought

I wanted someone young, a new love
to breathe into me another chance at living.
I wanted to feel. I wanted more time.

Out the window, a red bird. A white cloud.
A wedding party exiting a low building,
the bridesmaids in dresses of aquamarine.

The world a gilded box of jewels.
I couldn't take it, couldn't stop crying
on the bus. Why are we different

from the rest? That night I recited
to a roomful of strangers a poem
about a younger me, an older heartbreak

from a time when having a job
still seemed like fun. The next morning,
I stood in front of a seventeenth-century still life

of dead geese, cabbages, a quince
arranged in what the curator called
almost mathematical harmony.

Next to it, the decapitated head
of St. John the Baptist on a golden platter.
I was whelmed. I couldn't think.

I was despairing over someone
who said he saw no future with me.
Why did I even ask?

I walked through galleries
of moody photographs
and marble statues, stopping at a bronze shard

encased in a podium lit from above,
my face reflected in the glass.
Fragment of a Vessel, it read.

In the next room, I took a picture
of an impressionist painting, newly moved
by the sentimental strokes of pink and blue

churning against the sunset about to fall
over the city. I followed the light
toward the atrium, low din of footsteps

and chatter growing nearer
and clearer, like the rustle of a new lover
stirring awake beside me in summer.

Ordinary Pain

I took this city in bad faith, each stoplight a disaster.
Now the intersections are closures, the beginnings

of a four-leaf clover. When I miss you most acutely,
I first consult my diary: count the days since ovulation,

chart the course of PMS. *How much of me is woman
and how much of me was you?* I walk down aisle seven

cradling jars of pickled eggs, tinned sardines,
and olive oil, a baking dish I'll never use,

text messages I'll never send. I don't know what
I'm aching for, whether pregnancy or love, the mercy

that I never showed when you needed it the most.
How curious our lives which line the sidewalk

leading back. I thought tenderness was an indulgence
born from desires in the spleen. I mistake a yellow sock

for a marigold, a lawn sign for a swan. I press a hand
to a window and leave a child's print

behind. Small hands, numinous finger beds,
city of goddesses curling them shut.

The Day You Left, I Remembered

How the heart is a small windowpane
in a train speeding backward,   circling
one life from summer into spring
and into winter.
I watch the flora disappear
from the white noon,   trace your name
on the glassy muscle now brittle
from a cold which enters me, room

by room, my body freezing in sections
like the ice crusting
over Lake Mendota.
In waking life, I look out
onto a grassy courtyard
now bathed in snow,
invisible sun refracting
the ghost of autumn heat
which lit up our backs last year
and the year before that
when I lay in bed thinking
about how you told me
you loved me
while fucking me,
while loving me,
while fucking me,
the sky outside staggered   and drifting,
how I misread affection
for sadism,
sadism for ablution,
ablution for the thing
which scrubs one clean.

Dungeon Master

I.

I've lived not one life but many more.
I've wanted to leave, to exit this world,
but again I'm born into another moor,
this body bound by hands and feet by a lord
who condescends to me because I'm dumb,
can't learn, can't read between the lines I'm deigned
to memorize. Instead I chase a freedom
which does not set me free but leaves me stained
with sunspots, lines in places where they should
not cross, double digits between the brows,
descended down and ringed inside my body's wood,
eternal mark. Perpetual lark to think of how
I left my home to walk the Wall, to read Petrarch
as if I were some stranger to this dark.

II.

I was never a stranger to this dark,
locked inside a room with a television
projecting friends into my little ark:
Aurora, Cinderella, Ariel, and
me. One by one they found their destiny,
reclaiming what was theirs, as they were heirs
to a life, two legs, a man of royalty.
Retrieving fate is simple, needs no airs,
but I am heir to nothing, fettered
to this life to pay some debt I can't repair.
The Bible says the day you die is better
than the day that you were born. I dare
the prophets rise, come back to life ashore,
point to me what's good behind that final door.

III.

There's nothing good behind that final door,
same old shit, day in, day out, collecting
time stamps in our heads until there's no more
space on this receipt. I open credit
lines, finesse a score a little higher
than my SAT math score, which was perfect,
as was the life I pictured once for her.
But now I barely know her, no disrespect.
People change. Now I'm sitting at my desk
eating sardines, relinquishing that life,
each bite of bone, scale, and spiny flank
a gleaming Eucharist. Unhappy wife,
the house I make unfit for any patriarch,
just a wooden desk and me, writing in the dark.

IV.

This wooden desk where I write in the dark
grows crowded with pens and letters, books
by people lonely just like me. I mark
the company I keep, a line of cooks,
thieves, wives, and lovers for whom my letters
are no offense because they're dead, what's left
of them just words that see me, know me better
than any other, any mother, bereft
of any love not inked upon a page
or reel of videotape. Still I seek
a restitution, draw lines with sage
across my chest, an X, until it reeks
of desperation, song that doesn't slay
but flays, fey disaster of a prayer.

V.

I sing a fey disaster of a prayer
in a bid for God to grant me clemency.
I've bought indulgences, had cheap affairs,
confess I've weaponized my beauty
to use a man for more than money.
Let me prove I've changed, shed the ugly skins
whose thickness once protected me from being
true to you. I can atone, erase my sins,
change my life through which the Fates once wove this
wreck, unfurl the threads that cursed me in this
life, but not the next. I cut the scroll which spells
my death, end the cycle of this mess,
rewrite the trope, recode the DNA,
but salvation only comes halfway.

VI.

Salvation only comes halfway.
What's done is done. There are things that cannot
be undone though time inclines in bastard ways,
ballet of Hollywood and science, knot
of simulation, blackened mirror of
a bardo out of which we can't escape.
Someone on TV says that *time is a*
flat circle, which leaves my mouth agape
until I learned that it was Nietzsche,
not Matthew McConaughey, who said, *Your whole life,*
like a sand-glass, will always be reversed and
will ever run out again. What mortal strife
that God is dead yet thirsty still to dare
us to be free, to escape from this nightmare.

VII.

We're not free, won't escape from this nightmare,
endless scroll of TikTok and Instagram
where young women with no vaginal tears
gleam from all angles as if holograms.
Suddenly I'm in my thirties, living
in a city where twenty-five degrees
is cause for celebration, wishing
on a star whose radiance deceives
the heavens. For meager pay, I teach children
who condescend to me because I'm poor,
can't earn, can't part my hair along the line
that separates the cool from the abhorred.
And so I go from life to life to pay
this debt, each dawn another Groundhog Day.

VIII.

This debt, each dawn another Groundhog Day
of seeing owls, elk, and other strange
forms and swine, omens as if layaway
for some greater sign, stars to be arranged
into a pattern that can solve my life's
design. I see a psychoanalyst
who listens to me scream and cry, derives
a narrative for why I'm dead like this.
You could say that I have mommy issues,
like the sky is blue and water wet.
You could say that *she* had mommy issues,
the orgiastic lineage beset
upon this bloodline, cursed to cicatrize
each life, each file in the soul's archive.

IX.

Each life another file in the soul's archive,
rotation like a dirge, a Rolodex
of suffering, a samsara or five,
matrices of Zionists in latex
coats and sunglasses, running from a flock
of swans, agents of desire, actors
in a *Truman Show*, German black box
theater in which we cosplay martyrs.
I've seen the ways a man can freeze to death
and each of them was beautiful and holy,
quiet as the snow on Devil's Lake, breath
of nothing living but the ghosts that see
right through us, watching, hypnotized,
the reenactment of our dozen past lives.

X.

Cursed to reenact our dozen past lives,
each configured of different fathers,
different mothers, different husbands, wives,
and lovers, but still the lesson of another
was one I failed over and over.
Once I was a schoolteacher in a western
prairie town. I was handsome; so was my lover.
Of course we didn't learn our lesson.
He reincarnated as a recent lover
who matched with me on Tinder, sent me sex
toys in the mail and a Tom of Finland choker,
then told me I was too old, a Gen-X
to his millennial. I was born in 1985.
As I write this, I'm only thirty-five.

XI.

As I write this, I'm still thirty-five,
chimera of a girl and her mother,
the mind arrested, soul barely alive
from one heartbreak to another.
I tell myself that brighter days are coming
but I don't know how or when. Does it matter?
All girls deserve the kind of love I've only
seen on-screen, visions of Jacob's Ladder
leading to a perfect body, perfect teeth
which clamp, sharklike, on escargot and baguettes
but mostly cigarettes, my gray sheath
a mirror image of Carolyn Bessette's.
But alas. I'm no longer twenty-five.
No time to do it right, make it out alive.

XII.

No time to do it right, make it out alive,
though what's the use if I'm just spit back out
into this ostensible paradise
where the fruits of love's labor lie in doubt?
One swipe and you're out. Every man I date
is a Gemini, a twin flame until the
lights come on and he doesn't like my pate,
my poems, my panoramic worldview
that his narrow pupillary distance
eschews. I don't get it. I thought guys
liked features of neoteny, baby-faced
countenance, wide-set Bratz doll eyes.
I recuse myself from this diversion.
In the next life, I'll make another bargain.

XIII.

In the next life, I'll make another bargain,
earn my keep such that others weep out of
existential regret that they didn't
major in English, get an MFA,
live for three years, sexless, in Dairyland,
USA. My lover will be a home-
owner who makes good bread, writes in longhand,
does one-handed push-ups on the Driftless loam.
Out the window, a clear blue lake circled by black
sand freezes in summer, thaws in winter.
We live like this until we circle back
to one, live and die as one, return
to the rib of that primal garden.

XIV.

Returned to the rib of that primal garden
at last. No more suffering. No more breaths
where we rest in the skin of God's pardon:
death as if birth and birth as if death.
Gone is the weight of the world on my back
like a tramp stamp whose butterfly wings
can't fly me to space, debate fate with Shaq.
I'm cinder, I'm soot, cosmic shit of all things,
primordial dreck, sewage of Lethe,
the stains on my soul a quartz that divines
the nature of time: an endlessly
splintering tessellation of lives—
the private, the public, the chthonic lore.
I've lived not one life but many more.

XV.

I've lived not one life but many more.
I was never a stranger to this dark,
know there's nothing good behind that final door
but a wooden desk where I write in the dark.
I sing a fey disaster of a prayer
but salvation only comes halfway,
can't free me. There's no end to this nightmare,
this debt, each dawn another Groundhog Day,
each life another file in the soul's archive,
cursed to reenact our dozen past lives.
As I write this, I'm no longer thirty-five.
No time to do it right, make it out alive.
In the next life, I'll make another bargain:
meet my lover back in that primal garden.

Lullaby

Because it was April, the tree bore fruit.
I moved picture frames from room to room,
then back until the sun came up.
I closed my eyes and counted to five, then
it was June and the street was littered with apples.
We stack some squares and call this a house.
Celery, milk, bread, and cheese.
Summer fades into fall.
An old woman stops me to ask the time.
I like when old women are like Chinese almanacs.
I don't tell my mother about any of this.
I watch myself from a tree a little longer,
rustle the leaves until you look.

Acknowledgments

Some of these poems were previously published in the following journals:

Recliner: "Y2K" and "Ceremony"
The Yale Review: "Perfect"
Joyland: "Blindness Pattern"
Washington Square Review: "Feral Spice"
The Cortland Review: "Fragment of a Vessel," "Duty-Free," and "21st Century Pizza"

My endless gratitude to the editors for bringing them out into the world.

Many thanks to the Creative Writing Department at the University of Wisconsin–Madison for three years of generous support; to the Bread Loaf Writers' Conference for the indelible community of friends and writers it brought into my life; to Beth Dial and the National Poetry Series, whose work has been vital to the legacy of contemporary American poetry; to Solmaz Sharif, who, by choosing this manuscript, gave it life; to Allie Merola at Penguin for cultivating it into its final form; to Ryan Sullivan for amending all varieties of hyphens, commas, misspellings, and mathematical constants herein; and to the trees of Yahara Place Park, where I wrote most of these poems, and whose cottonwood and locust leaves will blanket the earth in every shade of red by the time this book comes out.

Notes

The final two lines of "Arrangements" are inspired by an image in a poem by Lucie Brock-Broido titled "Self-Portrait with Her Hair on Fire," which appears in her book *Trouble in Mind* (2004).

"Fragment of a Vessel" is named for the eponymous eighth-century BC Greek artifact in the Art Institute of Chicago, which also houses the other artworks referenced in the poem: *Still Life with Game Fowl* (ca. 1600–1603) by Juan Sánchez Cotán, *Salome with the Head of Saint John the Baptist* (ca. 1639–42) by Guido Reni, and *Stacks of Wheat (End of Summer)* (ca. 1890–91) by Claude Monet. The line "Why are we different / from the rest?" is from the poem "We Don't Know How to Say Goodbye" by Anna Akhmatova, translated from the Russian by Stanley Kunitz and Max Hayward.

A number of lines in "Punishment" make reference to or directly quote a lecture given by Karl Shoemaker in his class "The History of Punishment" at the University of Wisconsin–Madison, fall 2019.

In "Dungeon Master," references to Allen Mandelbaum's translations of Dante appear in Sonnet I, lines 4–6 (*Paradiso*, IV: 43–45), Sonnet VII, lines 8–9 (*Paradiso*, XIII: 4–6), and Sonnet XIII, lines 9–10 (*Inferno*, XXXII: 22–24); Sonnet IV, lines 4–5 are taken from the title of the film *The Cook, the Thief, His Wife, and Her Lover* (1989), directed by Peter Greenaway; and Sonnet VI, lines 7–12 quote *True Detective*, season 1, episode 5 and Nietzsche's *The Gay Science: Book IV*, §341.

GAROUS ABDOLMALEKIAN: *Lean Against This Late Hour* ✳ **PAIGE ACKERSON-KIELY:** *Dolefully,*
A Rampart Stands ✳ **JOHN ASHBERY:** *Selected Poems; Self-Portrait in a Convex Mirror* ✳ **PAUL BEATTY:**
Joker, Joker, Deuce ✳ **JOSHUA BENNETT:** *Owed; The Sobbing School; The Study of Human Life*
✳ **TED BERRIGAN:** *The Sonnets* ✳ **LAUREN BERRY:** *The Lifting Dress* ✳ **JOE BONOMO:** *Installations* ✳
PHILIP BOOTH: *Lifelines: Selected Poems 1950–1999; Selves* ✳ **JIM CARROLL:** *Fear of Dreaming: The Selected*
Poems; Living at the Movies; Void of Course ✳ **SU CHO:** *The Symmetry of Fish* ✳ **ADRIENNE CHUNG:**
Organs of Little Importance ✳ **RIO CORTEZ:** *Golden Ax* ✳ **ALISON HAWTHORNE DEMING:** *Genius Loci;*
Rope; Stairway to Heaven ✳ **CARL DENNIS:** *Another Reason; Callings; Earthborn; New and Selected Poems*
1974–2004; Night School; Practical Gods; Ranking the Wishes; Unknown Friends ✳ **DIANE DI PRIMA:**
Loba ✳ **STUART DISCHELL:** *Backwards Days; Dig Safe* ✳ **STEPHEN DOBYNS:** *Velocities: New and*
Selected Poems 1966–1992 ✳ **EDWARD DORN:** *Way More West* ✳ **HEID E. ERDRICH:** *Little Big Bully* ✳
ROGER FANNING: *The Middle Ages* ✳ **ADAM FOULDS:** *The Broken Word: An Epic Poem of the British*
Empire in Kenya, and the Mau Mau Uprising Against It ✳ **CARRIE FOUNTAIN:** *Burn Lake; Instant Winner;*
The Life ✳ **AMY GERSTLER:** *Dearest Creature; Ghost Girl; Index of Women; Medicine; Nerve Storm;*
Scattered at Sea ✳ **EUGENE GLORIA:** *Drivers at the Short-Time Motel; Hoodlum Birds; My Favorite*
Warlord; Sightseer in This Killing City ✳ **DEBORA GREGER:** *In Darwin's Room* ✳ **ZEINA HASHEM BECK:**
O ✳ **TERRANCE HAYES:** *American Sonnets for My Past and Future Assassin; Hip Logic; How to Be Drawn;*
Lighthead; So to Speak; Wind in a Box ✳ **NATHAN HOKS:** *The Narrow Circle* ✳ **ROBERT HUNTER:**
Sentinel and Other Poems ✳ **MARY KARR:** *Viper Rum* ✳ **WILLIAM KECKLER:** *Sanskrit of the Body* ✳
JACK KEROUAC: *Book of Blues; Book of Haikus; Book of Sketches* ✳ **JOANNA KLINK:** *Circadian;*
Excerpts from a Secret Prophecy; The Nightfields; Raptus ✳ **JOANNE KYGER:** *As Ever: Selected Poems* ✳
ANN LAUTERBACH: *Door; Hum; If in Time: Selected Poems 1975–2000; On a Stair; Or to Begin Again;*
Spell; Under the Sign ✳ **CORINNE LEE:** *Plenty; Pyx* ✳ **PHILLIS LEVIN:** *May Day; Mr. Memory & Other*
Poems ✳ **PATRICIA LOCKWOOD:** *Motherland Fatherland Homelandsexuals* ✳ **WILLIAM LOGAN:** *Rift*
of Light ✳ **J. MICHAEL MARTINEZ:** *Museum of the Americas; Tarta Americana* ✳ **ADRIAN MATEJKA:**
The Big Smoke; Map to the Stars; Mixology; Somebody Else Sold the World ✳ **MICHAEL MCCLURE:**
Huge Dreams: San Francisco and Beat Poems ✳ **ROSE MCLARNEY:** *Forage; Its Day Being Gone* ✳
DAVID MELTZER: *David's Copy: The Selected Poems of David Meltzer* ✳ **TERESA K. MILLER:**
Borderline Fortune ✳ **ROBERT MORGAN:** *Dark Energy; Terroir* ✳ **CAROL MUSKE-DUKES:** *Blue Rose;*
An Octave Above Thunder: New and Selected Poems; Red Trousseau; Twin Cities ✳ **ALICE NOTLEY:**
Certain Magical Acts; Culture of One; The Descent of Alette; Disobedience; For the Ride; In the Pines;
Mysteries of Small Houses ✳ **WILLIE PERDOMO:** *The Crazy Bunch; The Essential Hits of Shorty Bon Bon*
✳ **DANIEL POPPICK:** *Fear of Description* ✳ **LIA PURPURA:** *It Shouldn't Have Been Beautiful* ✳
LAWRENCE RAAB: *The History of Forgetting; Visible Signs: New and Selected Poems* ✳ **BARBARA RAS:**
The Last Skin; One Hidden Stuff ✳ **MICHAEL ROBBINS:** *Alien vs. Predator; The Second Sex; Walkman*
✳ **PATTIANN ROGERS:** *Flickering; Generations; Holy Heathen Rhapsody; Quickening Fields; Wayfare*
✳ **SAM SAX:** *Madness* ✳ **ROBYN SCHIFF:** *Information Desk: An Epic; A Woman of Property* ✳
WILLIAM STOBB: *Absentia; Nervous Systems* ✳ **TRYFON TOLIDES:** *An Almost Pure Empty Walking*
✳ **VINCENT TORO:** *Tertulia* ✳ **PAUL TRAN:** *All the Flowers Kneeling* ✳ **SARAH VAP:** *Viability* ✳
ANNE WALDMAN: *Gossamurmur; Kill or Cure; Manatee/Humanity; Trickster Feminism* ✳ **JAMES WELCH:**
Riding the Earthboy 40 ✳ **PHILIP WHALEN:** *Overtime: Selected Poems* ✳ **PHILLIP B. WILLIAMS:**
Mutiny ✳ **ROBERT WRIGLEY:** *Anatomy of Melancholy and Other Poems; Beautiful Country; Box;*
Earthly Meditations: New and Selected Poems; Lives of the Animals; Reign of Snakes; The True Account
of Myself as a Bird ✳ **MARK YAKICH:** *The Importance of Peeling Potatoes in Ukraine; Spiritual Exercises;*
Unrelated Individuals Forming a Group Waiting to Cross